Seasons Around You

Winter

Saviour Pirotta

WAYLAND

Seasons Around You

 Autumn    Spring

Summer   Winter

Cover photograph: Building a snowman.

Title page: Wrapped up warmly for winter.

Produced for Wayland Publishers Limited by
Roger Coote Publishing
Gissing's Farm, Fressingfield
Eye, Suffolk IP21 5SH, England

Series designer: Jan Stirling
Book designer: Victoria Webb

First published in 1998 by
Wayland Publishers Limited
61 Western Road, Hove
East Sussex BN3 1JD, England

Find Wayland on the Internet at http://www.wayland.co.uk

British Library Cataloguing in Publication Data
Pirotta, Saviour, 1958–
   Winter. – (Seasons around you)
   1.Winter – Pictorial works – Juvenile literature
   I. Title
   508.2

   ISBN 0 7502 2277 8

Printed and bound by EuroGrafica, Vicenza, Italy.

Picture acknowledgements
Bubbles 8 (Jennie Woodcock); Eye Ubiquitous 6
(Tim Hawkins), 25 (Paul Thompson); FLPA 12
(T Whittaker), 18 (RP Lawrence), 19 (MJ Thomas),
20 (MJ Thomas), 21 (AJ Roberts); Getty Images front
cover (Lori Adamski Peek), 4 (Connie Coleman), 10
(Chad Ehlers), 11 (Gary Holscher), 16 (Lori Adamski
Peek), 17 (Lori Adamski Peek), 23 (Peter Cade); Image
Bank 9 (Benn Mitchell), 14 (Patti McConville), 27 (Gary
Farber); Impact 26 (Brian Harris), 28 (Jeremy Nicholl);
Life File 15 (Emma Lee); Peter Sanders 29; TWP/Tim
Woodcock 22, 24; Wayland Picture Library 5, 7;
Zefa 13 (Fritz Bergmann).

Contents

Words that appear in **bold** are explained in the glossary on page 32.

Winter is here

What do you notice about winter?
The weather is very cold and you can
see your breath in the air.

We wear thick, warm clothes.
Jumpers, coats, hats, gloves and
scarves keep out the cold.

Wet weather clothes

It rains a lot in winter.
Sometimes there are
big puddles in the street.

When it rains, we put on boots and raincoats. Umbrellas help us keep dry.

Winter food

Hot food helps keep us warm.
We eat stew or baked potatoes with
hot fillings.

It's cold working outdoors. People drink soup or hot drinks out of **thermos flasks**.

Icy weather

When it gets very cold, water freezes.
Lakes and streams turn to ice.

Long, shiny icicles hang from
tree branches and drainpipes.

Beware of the ice

Puddles on the road can turn to ice.
It is very dangerous. Cars can skid
on the ice.

Road gritters scatter sand over icy roads to make them less slippery.

13

Here comes the snow

Sometimes it snows in winter.
Outdoors, almost everything turns white.

If the snow is very deep, children cannot go to school. Some people have to dig their way out of their houses.

Winter games

It's fun when it snows. We can build snowmen and have snowball fights.

Some people go sledging or skating.
Others go skiing in the mountains.

Animals in winter

Most animals do not like the cold. Dormice **hibernate** in their nests all through the winter.

It's cold out in the fields.
Sheep grow thicker coats to
keep them warm.

On the farm

In winter, farmers spend less time working on the land. Instead they mend fences, walls, barns and farm machinery.

Cows are kept in barns,
out of the cold and the rain.

Christmas is coming

In December, we get ready for Christmas. At school we sing carols and perform the **nativity play**.

At home we put up decorations.
People send Christmas cards to all their
friends and buy each other presents.

Happy Christmas!

It's Christmas Day! We gather round the Christmas tree and open our presents.

Christmas dinner is a big meal.
We have turkey with **stuffing**,
followed by Christmas pudding.

A new year begins

After Christmas we celebrate New Year. People go to parties and make special promises, called **resolutions**.

In December, there is a Jewish festival called **Hanukah**. People light a special candle called a menorah.

More festivals

Soon it is time for **Chinese New Year**. There are street celebrations and an exciting dragon dance.

Muslims celebrate the festival of **Id-ul-Fitr**.
There is a feast with lots of food.

Winter activities

 GEOGRAPHY

Effects of weather on people and their surroundings What would you do for fun if the weather were really hot? What would you eat and drink?

What would you do if the weather were really cold? Would you choose to eat and drink the same foods?

Comparing localities Make a report, describing your local neighbourhood in winter. Include the weather, type of food available in the shops, clothes people are wearing and vegetation in the park or local gardens.

Now contrast this with winter (the coolest season) in a hot country. Is the weather the same? Do people wear the same clothes? Do they eat the same food?

Land and buildings Draw pictures of the various buildings mentioned in this book. What is each building used for?

 SCIENCE

Using pictures from clothes catalogues and old magazines, make a collage of winter clothes. What do they all have in common?

Life processes Look at the animals in this book. Why do some of them hibernate in burrows and nests and others grow thicker coats? What do human beings do to keep warm?

Electricity Look at the pictures in the book and list those that use electricity. Imagine there was a power cut and think how it would affect what is happening in the picture.

Humans as organisms Using pictures from clothes catalogues, make a collage of winter clothes. Label each item of clothing with its name and the part of the body that it keeps warm.

 MATHS

Understanding and using measures Make sweet bags for Id or Christmas celebrations. Ask your friends to weigh out equal amounts of sweets before wrapping them in coloured paper.

 ART

Use some of the ideas explored in the book to make Christmas cards. Which scenes are considered the most appropriate for Yuletide sentiments?

Copy the menorah on page 27 to design Hanukah cards.

Paint Chinese New Year greetings on paper banners and hang them around the school.

 RE

All the festivals in this book share a common theme: light as a symbol of hope and help. Tell the stories of Hanukah, Christmas and Id.

Make or obtain some foods that are eaten in every winter festival. Share them with the class.

Light a special Hanukah menorah in your class.

 DESIGN AND TECHNOLOGY

Design and make 'lucky money' envelopes for Chinese New Year. Paint them red (a lucky colour) and copy the Chinese character 'Fu' (meaning good luck and happiness) on to them.

 DANCE AND DRAMA

Write a nativity play or pantomime and perform it with your class.

Create a dance showing the story of Hanukah.

Find out about the story of Id and create a performance piece to show to other classes.

Topic web

ENGLISH
The Torah
Dickens's *A Christmas Carol*
Importance of correct sequence

GEOGRAPHY
Cold countries, hot countries
Environment: roads, forests,
  farms, cities
Change
Lands and buildings: farms,
  houses

ART
Cartoon strips: showing
  Christmas stories, snow scenes
Making Christmas cards,
  Hanukah and Id cards
Making packets for lucky
  money
Making Christmas decorations

SEASONS TOPIC WEB

DANCE AND DRAMA
Christmas play
The story of Hanukah
The story of Ramayana
Dragon dance

SCIENCE
Life processes: sleeping
  and waking
The weather
Ice and snow: freezing point
Wet and dry
Hot and cold
Rain and water
Food
Light and dark

RE
Christmas and Christianity
Hanukah candle
Diagram tables
Hanukah and Judaism
Celebrating Id-ul-Fitr
  and Islam

MATHS
Measuring and
  comparing hours
  of daylight
Measuring rainfall
Sequence of seasons

DESIGN AND TECHNOLOGY
Car safety
Mending fences

Resources

NON-FICTION
Weather Facts by P. Eden and C. Twist
(Dorling Kindersley, 1995)

Christmas by Clare Chandler (Wayland, 1996)

Chinese New Year by Sarah Moyse (Wayland, 1997)

Id-ul-Fitr by Kerena Marchant (Wayland, 1997)

Seasonal Crafts: Winter by Gillian Chapman
(Wayland, 1997)

Clothes in Hot and Cold Places by Simon Crisp
(Wayland, 1996)

Winter on the Farm by Janet Fitzgerald (Evans, 1995)

The Seasons by Debbie MacKinnon (Frances
Lincoln, 1995)

The World of Festivals by Philip Steele (Macdonald
Young Books, 1996)

FICTION AND POETRY
Winter Story by Jill Barklem (Collins Brambly
Hedge series, 1980). The adventures of the mice of
Brambly Hedge, with illustrations showing the
countryside in Winter.

Poems for Winter by Robert Hull (Wayland, 1995).
Seasonal poems from around the world, illustrated
with colour photographs.

Glossary

Burrows Holes in the ground made by animals to live in.

Chinese New Year The festival in January or February when Chinese people celebrate the start of a new year.

Hanukah A Jewish festival of light, celebrating the day when a group of Jews won the holy temple back from their Syrian enemy.

Hibernate To sleep through the winter.

Id-ul-Fitr A Muslim festival with a feast.

Nativity play A play about the birth of Jesus.

Resolutions Promises.

Road gritters Special vehicles that spread sand on icy roads to make them less slippery.

Stuffing Minced food put inside a chicken or a turkey.

Thermos flasks Containers that keep drinks or soup hot.

Index